4

AF529352

SHINY AND HER WARDROBE OF VIRTUES

PATIENCE

THE ABILITY TO STAY CALM AND WAIT WHEN THERE IS A DELAY

BY

Sukanya Shah

First published by Birch Books 2020

ISBN - 978-81-949495-8-9

Email : books.birch@gmail.com

To Adyana.
My first. My all.
May you always be more.

From the Author's Desk

Cossetted in our homes during the thick of the Covid-19 pandemic, I made every effort to keep my toddler happy and engaged. It made me wonder about the true legacy in learning that my child will bequeath. I cannot wait to pass on this treasure of a less than perfect world to her… one that will astonish her most often, teach her most definitely and hold her to two constants—challenge and change.

Shiny And Her Wardrobe Of Virtues was born of this sentiment. Shiny is a spritely little girl who owns a magical wardrobe, with virtuous items that on adorning, change her world view…virtues that go beyond the classroom and make her feel happy and whole.

I enjoyed writing these stories of gratitude, kindness, confidence, patience and love…but more so, I enjoyed diving into these most beautiful emotions and feelings with my child.

I hope you do too.

Love,
Sukanya.

It was a sunny Sunday in Shiny's town,
In her favourite pyjamas, she came prancing down.

At the breakfast table, she was bright and awake,
Awaiting her favourite, fluffy pancakes.

Vanilla pancakes were a Sunday special,
The batter was ready, beside the whistling kettle.

"Oh no," said mummy, we have to wait,
"We ran out of milk, the milkman is late!"

Shiny was restless, she wanted to eat.
It was Sunday after all, she'd waited all week.

She saw the clock ticking, her tummy growled.
Restless and ravenous, around the kitchen she prowled.

"I'm hungry,
Mummy!"

She mumbled and muttered, tapping the fork on her plate,
Said Daddy to Shiny, "Good things come to those who wait".

Just then her pyjamas, glistened and gleamed.
Her pyjamas of patience, had magic in their seams.

She suddenly felt better, she smiled and looked calm,
Just then came the milkman, waving his arm.

Sorry I'm late!"
MILK

Shiny was excited, Shiny was thrilled, Mummy added the milk, the ladle was filled.

MAPLE SYRUP

Hot off the hob, the pancakes were delicious.
The reward of waiting, was worthwhile and precious.

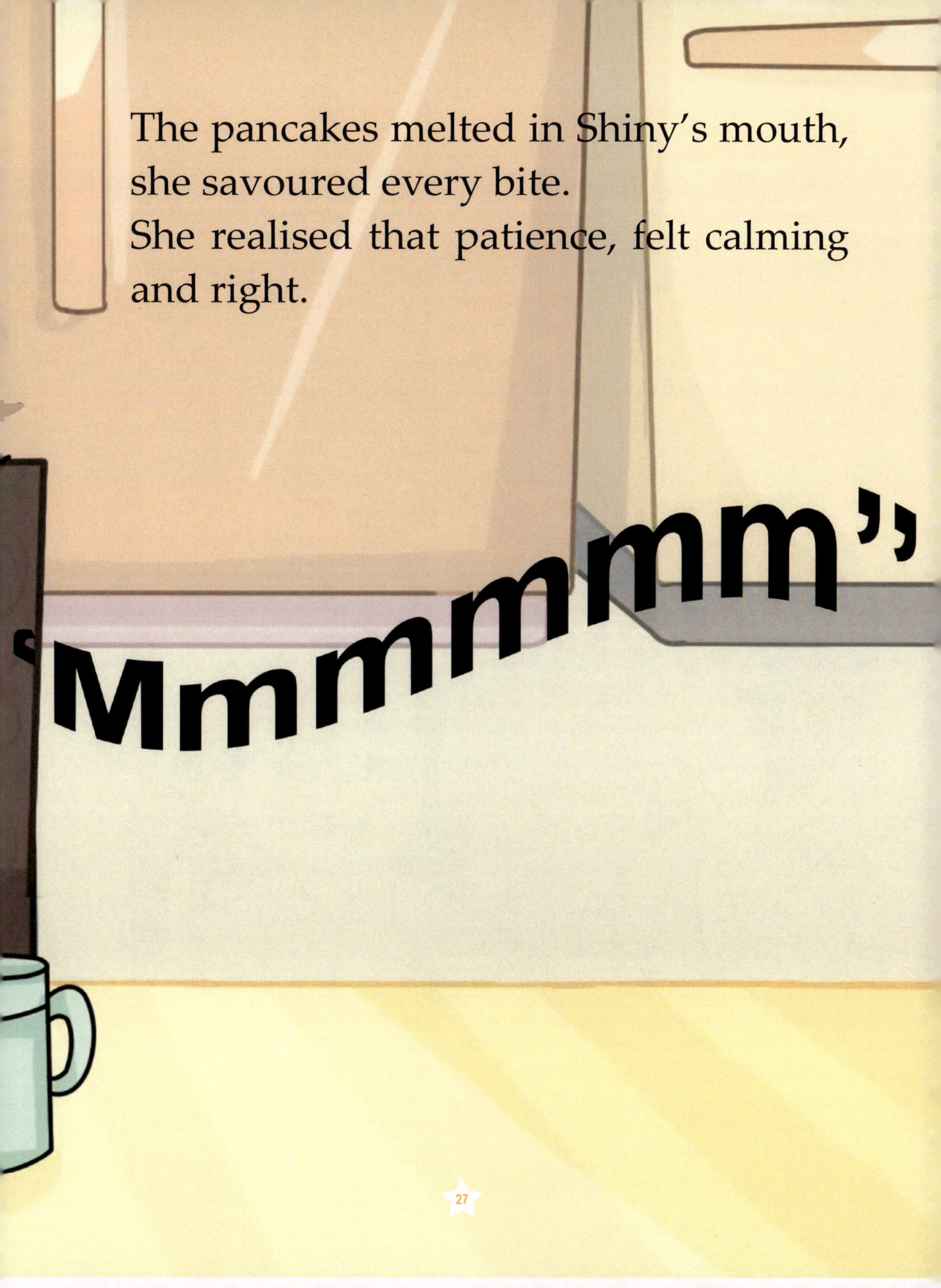

The pancakes melted in Shiny's mouth, she savoured every bite.
She realised that patience, felt calming and right.

'Mmmmmmm''

Said Mummy and Daddy, "You did so well!".
"It wasn't easy waiting", they could tell.

To be patient is to wait, to let time go by,
Shiny's pyjamas of patience, surely made
time fly!

Talking points for parents:

- Tell your child about a time you waited eagerly on something.
- Tell them how wonderful the outcome felt.
- Remind your child of an instance he/she was impatient and how waiting patiently may have helped.
- Explain these words and their feelings:

Restless / Calm

Delay / Hasten

Wait / Rush

- Teach your child to tell time.